Making Wise Investments

How to Gain an Everlasting Reward

Andy Sochor

Gospel Armory PUBLISHING

Published by:
Gospel Armory Publishing
Bowling Green, Kentucky
www.GospelArmory.com

Printed in the United States of America

ISBN: 978-1-942036-01-2

Table of Contents

"Do not work for the food which perishes,
but for the food which endures to eternal life..."
John 6:27

Introduction

Many people have a great interest in making investments that will help them gain wealth and secure their future in this life. While we should certainly be good stewards of the physical blessings we receive from God, this is not the type of investing we will be considering in this study. Instead, we will look at investments that are far more valuable and important than those that pertain to this life. The Bible speaks of investments we are to make that are of a *spiritual* nature. These are the investments we will discuss in this series.

~1~
The Value of the Soul

The first valuable commodity that we will consider in our study is the soul. People often fail to properly consider the value of their soul because their estimation is distorted by either self-deprecation (failing to see how valuable they are personally) or short-sightedness (failing to see past the things of this life). So let us see what the Scriptures teach us about the value of the soul.

> "*Then Jesus said to His disciples, 'If anyone wishes to come after Me, he must deny himself, and take up his cross and follow Me. For whoever wishes to save his life will lose it; but whoever loses his life for My sake will find it. For what will it profit a man if he gains the whole world and forfeits his soul? Or what will a man give in exchange for his soul?*" (Matthew 16:24-26).

Natural Desire for Self-Preservation

It is natural that man would rather save his life than lose it. This natural inclination toward caring for one's physical life is used by Paul to emphasize the need for husbands to demonstrate a sacrificial love for their wives: "*So husbands ought also to love their own wives as their own bodies. He who loves his own wife loves himself; for no one ever hated his own flesh, but nourishes and cherishes it, just as*

Christ also does the church" (Ephesians 5:28-29).

Although the desire for self-preservation is natural, Jesus says that one must learn to *"deny himself"* and be willing to *"lose...his life"* (Matthew 16:24-25). But why would anyone do this? It is not because Jesus is demanding the neglect or destruction of oneself. As we will notice in a later point, we are much too valuable in the Lord's eyes to adopt that mentality and behavior. Instead, Jesus says we must deny self and be willing to lose our lives in order to gain long-term security. Our desire for self-preservation should be more for our soul – our entire existence that extends past our time on earth – than our temporary physical lives.

Dangers of an Overly Ambitious Attitude

In this passage, Jesus warned against having an overly ambitious attitude. Though one may gain *"the whole world,"* it is meaningless if he *"forfeits his soul"* in the process (Matthew 16:26). Of course, we are not to completely shun ambition to the point of laziness (cf. 2 Thessalonians 3:10). In the parable of the talents, Jesus condemned the servant who so severely lacked ambition that he would not even put his master's money in the bank to earn interest on it (Matthew 25:24-28). At the same time, He praised those who went out and doubled their master's money that had been entrusted to them (Matthew 25:14-17, 19-23).

Rather than condemning ambition, Jesus condemned the attitude in which one is *never satisfied*. He asked the question: *"For what will it profit a man if he gains the whole world and forfeits his soul?"* (Matthew 16:26). However, no one will ever be able to gain the whole world. Yet this is the pursuit in which many are engaged. They may not say that their goal is to obtain the world. But there is a never-ending list of wants and desires that they have. Whenever they gain anything, that fulfilled desire is simply replaced in their minds with an unfulfilled desire. Regardless of their circumstances, they are never satisfied and always wanting *more*.

While a degree of ambition is good (cf. Ecclesiastes 9:10; Colossians 3:23), it must be tempered by *contentment*. Paul said, *"I have learned to be content in whatever circumstances I am"* (Philippians 4:11). This included both prosperity and poverty (Philippians 4:12). Paul was certainly a hard worker – even to the point of *"working night and day"* (2 Thessalonians 3:8) – but he understood the need to be content with just the basic necessities of life (1 Timothy 6:7-8).

In the parable of the rich land owner, Jesus described one who had an overly ambitious attitude. When he had a harvest greater than he expected, this man said, *"I will tear down my barns and build larger ones, and there I will store all my grain and my goods. And I will say to my soul, 'Soul, you have many goods laid up for many years to come; take your ease, eat, drink and be merry'"* (Luke 12:18-19). The productivity of his land did not make him a sinner. His plan to build larger barns was not inherently wrong. His sin was that he sought to gain more material goods by neglecting the well-being of his soul. He was called a *fool* because he forfeited his soul to gain the things of the world. He did not appreciate the value of his soul.

The Value of One's Soul

So that we do not make the same costly mistake as the rich man, we need to be sure we understand how valuable our souls are. First of all, our souls are valuable because they were *created by God*. In the beginning, God *"formed man of dust from the ground, and breathed into his nostrils the breath of life; and man became a living being [soul, KJV]"* (Genesis 2:7). Though the word in this verse simply denotes *breath* – the physical life that man and animals have in common – man is unique, having been made in the image of God (Genesis 1:27). God is the *"Father of spirits"* (Hebrews 12:9) and one day, every *"spirit will return to God who gave it"* (Ecclesiastes 12:7).

Second, our souls are valuable because they are the only thing we have than no one can take away from us. The things we possess in this life can be taken if *"thieves break in and steal"* (Matthew 6:19). Our souls, in contrast, cannot be taken from us. They were given to us by God and will be returned to Him in the end (Ecclesiastes 12:7). Paul told Timothy, *"For we have brought nothing into the world, so we cannot take anything out of it either"* (1 Timothy 6:7). Though everything in this life is only temporary (2 Peter 3:10; 1 John 2:17), our souls – which will live on after this life – are eternal (Matthew 25:46).

The words of Peter remind us just how valuable our souls are when he explained what it cost in order to secure our redemption: *"Knowing that you were not redeemed with perishable things like silver or gold from your futile way of life inherited from your forefathers, but with precious blood, as of a lamb unblemished and spotless, the blood of Christ"* (1 Peter 1:18-19). Jesus was God's *"only begotten Son"* (John 3:16).

The Father had to "*see*" His Son suffer a cruel and torturous death on the cross in order to make atonement for our sins (Isaiah 53:4-11). As Peter pointed out, the blood Jesus shed in His death was worth more than silver and gold. God would not have allowed His Son to endure what He did on the cross if our souls were of little value.

For these reasons, our souls are more valuable than anything and everything that exists in the world. This is why Jesus presented the question: "*For what will it profit a man if he gains the whole world and forfeits his soul?*" (Matthew 16:26). The answer is implied in the question: There is no profit for trading our souls for the things of this world. Our souls – not just our temporal physical lives, but our entire existence – must be valued above all the riches of this life.

What Happens if We Forfeit Our Soul?

Jesus made it clear that if we forfeit our souls for anything in this life, we have made a terrible decision. He showed us what the better choice is – diligently working to preserve our souls rather than neglecting our spiritual well-being in order to try and preserve, for a limited period of time, the things of this life.

If we make this failed investment – sacrificing our souls for the things of the world – we will not be able to give anything to buy it back. This is Jesus' point in His second question: "*Or what will a man give in exchange for his soul?*" (Matthew 16:26). One day, all of those who are lost will realize their error when they face the punishment for their sins – "*eternal destruction, away from the presence of the Lord and from the glory of His power*" (2 Thessalonians 1:9).

They will stand before the One who is *"able to destroy both soul and body in hell"* (Matthew 10:28), and will be told, *"Depart from Me, accursed ones, into the eternal fire which has been prepared for the devil and his angels"* (Matthew 25:41). At this point, there will be no hope. Even if one *"gains the whole world"* (Matthew 16:26), because his soul is more valuable than all of it, he will have nothing to offer to save himself in the end.

Conclusion

One day the Lord will return in judgment (2 Corinthians 5:10). At that time, He will *"repay every man according to his deeds"* (Matthew 16:27). Because our souls are so much more valuable than anything in this life, we must not risk losing our souls by not being in a state of readiness. Therefore, let us remember what Paul told the brethren in Thessalonica: *"The day of the Lord will come just like a thief in the night"* (1 Thessalonians 5:2). *"So then let us not sleep as others do, but let us be alert and sober"* (1 Thessalonians 5:6).

If we are to make wise investments to secure our future, we must start by recognizing the need to take care of our souls.

Questions for Discussion & Reflection

1. What often causes people to improperly consider the value of their soul?

2. Explain the desire for self-preservation and how it can be properly used by Christians.

3. By what must ambition be tempered? Why?

4. In Jesus' parable of the rich land owner (Luke 12:16-21), explain how this man sinned and why he was called a fool.

5. Why are our souls valuable?

6. Why is it a poor investment for one to trade his soul for the world?

~2~
Buy the Truth

Our first lesson dealt with the value of the soul. Without understanding this, the other points in our study are useless. But now that we understand the value of the soul, how should we care for our soul? In this lesson, we will consider the importance of possessing the truth.

> *"Buy truth, and do not sell it, get wisdom and instruction and understanding"* (Proverbs 23:23).

What Is Truth?

The above question was what Pilate asked Jesus. When Jesus told the governor that He came *"to testify to the truth"* (John 18:37), Pilate responded with the question, *"What is truth?"* (John 18:38). The irony in his question was that he asked the One who was the embodiment of truth, as Jesus told His disciples earlier, *"I am...the truth"* (John 14:6).

Since Jesus is *"the truth"* (John 14:6) and He was the Word of God in the flesh (John 1:14), then we should also understand that the word of God written down in the Scriptures is the truth. When Jesus prayed to the Father before His death, He said, *"Your word is truth"* (John 17:17). The words of the psalmist remind us that *"the sum of* [God's] *word is truth"* (Psalm 119:160).

So what is truth? It is the message that has been delivered to us by God. In Christ – and therefore, in His word (cf. John 1:14) – *"are hidden all the treasures of wisdom and knowledge"* (Colossians 2:3). David wrote that the words of God are *"more desirable than gold, yes, than much fine gold"* (Psalm 19:10).

What the Truth Gives Us

Why is the truth of God's word *"more desirable than gold"* (Psalm 19:10)? Why are we told to *"buy truth"* and *"not sell it"* (Proverbs 23:23)? Truth is so valuable because of what we get from it – *"wisdom and instruction and understanding"* (Proverbs 23:23). Let us briefly consider each one of these.

Understanding – Through God's word we are able to have *understanding*. David wrote, *"I understand more than the aged, because I have observed Your precepts"* (Psalm 119:100). The truth of God's word is simple enough that all can understand. When Jesus taught, *"the common people heard him gladly"* (Mark 12:37, KJV). Those who possess worldly wisdom to the point of arrogance see the simple message of the gospel as *"foolishness"* (1 Corinthians 1:23). But God purposely made His word simple so that it could be understood by all (Ephesians 3:4). By looking to His word, we can *"understand what the will of the Lord is"* (Ephesians 5:17) and know the difference between right and wrong (Psalm 119:104).

Instruction – The word of God is also valuable because it provides *instructions* regarding how we must live our lives.

This is important because of what we studied in our previous lesson about the value of the soul. After teaching that one's soul is more valuable than anything in this world, Jesus said that one day He will *"repay every man according to his deeds"* (Matthew 16:27). How can we make sure our deeds are right so that we might be prepared for this judgment? We must look to the *instructions* of God's word. The word of God shows what is required of us (Colossians 3:18-4-6; *et al.*). It also contains instruction warning us of what we should *not* do (Colossians 3:5-9; *et al.*).

Wisdom – In addition to the *understanding* and *instruction* found in the word of God, the truth is also able to provide *wisdom*. The psalmist said, *"Your commandments make me wiser than my enemies"* (Psalm 119:98). The simplest definition for wisdom is the ability to properly *apply* knowledge. Once we understand the instructions that God has given us in His word, we must practice them. James said we must be *"doers of the word, and not merely hearers"* (James 1:22). Our experience in practicing the things taught in the word of God causes us to grow in wisdom (Hebrews 5:14). Knowledge alone is not enough; belief is not enough; we must live according to the precepts that have been revealed to us from God.

The Cost of Truth

To *buy* the truth implies that there is a price we must pay. Acquiring truth is not just about what we *get* (wisdom, instruction, and understanding), it is also about what we must *give up*. But even with this, it is still a wise investment to give up whatever is necessary in order to obtain the truth. But what sort of things must we be willing to give up?

Pride – To buy the truth often means admitting that we were wrong. Therefore, we need humility when we engage in a study of the Scriptures. James said that *"in humility"* we are to *"receive the word"* (James 1:21). But not only must we not take pride in our own limited understanding, we are not to take pride in traditions, preachers, churches, etc. It could be that the traditions in which we take pride are contrary to God's word and render our worship vain (Matthew 15:6-9). It might be that the preachers in which we place our trust are in error and need to be corrected (Acts 18:24-26; Galatians 2:11-14). Or perhaps the church with which we worship has *"a name that* [it is] *alive, but* [it is] *dead"* (Revelation 3:1). In every way, we must humbly submit to the will of God and conform our beliefs, teachings, and practices to the truth that we find in the Scriptures.

Time and effort – While God's word is understandable (Ephesians 3:4), we are not born with an understanding of it. We must *study* in order to learn how to *"accurately* [handle] *the word of truth"* (2 Timothy 2:15). This must be a continual process in which we grow and mature in our understanding of the will of God. We must *"give attention to reading"* (1 Timothy 4:13, NKJV) so that we might *"grow in the grace and knowledge of our Lord and Savior Jesus Christ"* (2 Peter 3:18). As the noble-minded Bereans, we should study the Scriptures daily so that we might develop an understanding of God's word (Acts 17:11). We must be willing to devote the time and effort necessary to learn the truth.

Friends and family – Sadly, buying the truth often puts one at odds with others who refuse to accept the truth themselves. Jesus warned His apostles that the world would *hate* them (John 15:18-19). Peter warned Christians to "*not be surprised at the fiery ordeal*" which was going to come upon them (1 Peter 4:12). This trouble to which he referred was not the general hardships of life that all men must endure. Instead, they were going to suffer "*as a Christian*" (1 Peter 4:16). Jesus even warned that the opposition we face for following Him will sometimes come from those who are the closest to us. "*A man's enemies will be the members of his household*" (Matthew 10:36). We may have to sacrifice certain relationships in this life for the sake of the truth.

Why Some Sell the Truth

To sell the truth is to compromise it or even abandon it altogether. Why do some choose to do this? Jesus gives us an answer in the following passage:

> "*Enter through the narrow gate; for the gate is wide and the way is broad that leads to destruction, and there are many who enter through it. For the gate is small and the way is narrow that leads to life, and there are few who find it*" (Matthew 7:13-14).

Jesus said that the way of error is *easier* and *more popular* than the way of truth. Sadly, many are short-sighted and choose the ease and popularity of the broad way. Peter said that those who do not continue to grow as they should are "*short-sighted, having forgotten* [their] *purification from* [their] *former sins*" (2 Peter 1:9). We must not sell the truth – either through compromise or outright abandonment of it – for the truth is "*a lamp to* [our] *feet*" (Psalm 119:105) that shows us the safe way down the narrow path that leads to life.

Conclusion

We must buy the truth and never sell it. We must allow it to guide us in all that we do. We must teach it to those who will listen and defend it against error. Why is it so important that we do these things? It is because the truth contained in God's word is *"more desirable than gold, yes, than much fine gold"* (Psalm 19:10).

Only the truth found in Scripture is able to provide us with *"wisdom and instruction and understanding"* (Proverbs 23:23) in things pertaining to God. Let us always remember the value of truth and be committed to doing what is necessary in order to obtain it.

Questions for Discussion & Reflection

1. Explain the answer to Pilate's question: "What is truth?"

2. What does the truth contained in God's word help us to understand?

3. Explain the importance of God's instructions as it relates to the final judgment.

4. How does the truth help us gain wisdom?

5. What does the truth cost us?

6. Why might it be tempting to "sell" the truth?

~3~
The Pearl of Great Value

In the previous lesson, we considered the value of the truth – the word of God – and why we should buy it and not sell it. In this lesson, we will consider something so valuable that Jesus talked about the wisdom in one selling everything that he owned in order to buy it. The thing which He said was so valuable was the kingdom.

> "*Again, the kingdom of heaven is like a merchant seeking fine pearls, and upon finding one pearl of great value, he went and sold all that he had and bought it*" (Matthew 13:45-46).

What Is the Kingdom?

Many today are looking for a future, yet-to-be-established kingdom that Christ will set up when He returns. But this is not how the Bible describes the kingdom. Jesus came in order to "*set up a kingdom which will never be destroyed*" (Daniel 2:44). Did He fail to do what He planned to do? Certainly not! Those who believe that Jesus is going to set up a physical kingdom believe that He must do it when He returns because the Jews rejected Him from being their king the first time He was here. The Jews certainly did reject Him in the end; but if Jesus' purpose was to establish a physical kingdom, John recorded a time when the people were willing to *"take Him by force and make Him king"* (John 6:15). Besides this, He had the authority to call down *"more than twelve legions of angels"* (Matthew 26:53). If Jesus' mission was to establish a physical kingdom on the earth, He could have done so without the support of even one human follower.

But Jesus' kingdom is not *physical,* but *spiritual* in nature. Jesus told Pilate, *"My kingdom is not of this world"* (John 18:36). This kingdom is the church (Matthew 16:18-19). It is the body of the saved (Acts 2:47; Ephesians 5:23) – all those who have been *"rescued...from the domain of darkness, and transferred...to the kingdom of His beloved Son"* (Colossians 1:13).

The Importance of "Seeking"

The Bible repeatedly emphasizes the importance of *seeking.* Jesus said, *"Seek, and you will find"* (Matthew 7:7). The Hebrew writer said that God *"is a rewarder of those who seek Him"* (Hebrews 11:6). We cannot sit back idly and wait for God to reveal something to us – He has already revealed everything we need to know. *"Everything pertaining to life and godliness"* has been revealed *"through the true knowledge of Him who called us"* (2 Peter 1:3). *"All Scripture is inspired by God"* and is able to make *"the man of God...adequate"* (2 Timothy 3:16-17). But we must be *"diligent"* in *"handling the word of truth"* (2 Timothy 2:15).

The Scriptures provide us with a picture of the kingdom of God that Jesus called the *"pearl of great value"* (Matthew 13:46). We must be diligent in searching the Scriptures to learn about His kingdom and then be diligent in our quest to find it.

How Do We Know When We Have Found It?

If we are looking for something, it is important that we know what we are seeking. The man in Jesus' parable sold everything he owned in order to obtain the precious pearl. He did this because of the great value attached to this pearl (which represented the Lord's kingdom). We should have the same desire today. But it is vital that we find the Lord's kingdom (church, cf. Matthew 16:18-19) so that we do not waste everything on a cheap counterfeit. We need to be able to identify the Lord's kingdom (His church).

Universally, the kingdom is the body of the saved (Acts 2:47; Ephesians 5:23). Who are the saved? Many will try to lead you into a counterfeit church by proclaiming a different or incomplete plan of salvation than the one shown to us in the Scriptures. How are we saved? Not by faith alone (James 2:24). Not by simply claiming Jesus as Lord (Matthew 7:21-23). Those who are saved are those who **believe** (John 8:24), those who **repent** (Luke 13:3), those who **confess** (Romans 10:9-10), and those who are **baptized** (Mark 16:16; 1 Peter 3:21). Baptism is the entrance into the kingdom as God adds these individuals to the church (Acts 2:41, 47).

Locally, there are congregations made up of those who are saved. How do we identify a local church of Christ?

- **Name (symbol of allegiance)** – The church belongs to Christ (Matthew 16:18; Acts 20:28); therefore, it wears His name. The churches in the first century were not aligned with larger religious groups/denominations (as is the case with the Baptists, Methodists, etc.). They were simply *"churches of Christ"* (Romans 16:16).

- **Organization** – The New Testament describes local churches as being made up of *"overseers and deacons,"* and *"saints"* (Philippians 1:1). Elsewhere Paul mentioned *"evangelists," "pastors and teachers"* (Ephesians 4:11). Specific qualifications are given for elders (overseers/pastors) and deacons (1 Timothy 3:1-13; Titus 1:5-9). But beyond the local church, we read of *no other organization* in the New Testament – either a confederacy of churches (each church was *autonomous*; cf. 1 Peter 5:2) or a collective body of Christians engaged in some spiritual work.
- **Work** – The local church has been given two regular, on-going works: evangelism (1 Timothy 3:15; 1 Thessalonians 1:8) and edification (Ephesians 4:12, 16). Under certain, specific circumstances, the local church is also authorized to engage in benevolence for needy saints (Acts 4:34-35; 11:29-30; 1 Timothy 5:3-16). But nowhere in the New Testament has the local church been authorized to involve itself in the "social gospel" – entertainment, recreation, and other ways in which so many churches today try to cater to the desires of men.
- **Worship** – The Lord expects us to worship acceptably – *"in spirit and truth"* (John 4:24). What are we to *do* in our assemblies? We must do what we see the first century church doing – singing and praying (1 Corinthians 14:15), preaching (1 Corinthians 14:26; Acts 20:7), observing the Lord's Supper (Acts 20:7; 1 Corinthians 11:20-34), and taking up the collection (1 Corinthians 16:1-2). We do not find

authority for instrumental music, plays, testimonials, and other acts that are commonly found in the assemblies of the churches of men.

We seek the kingdom by doing what is necessary in order to gain entrance into the kingdom (belief, repentance, confession, and baptism). After doing that, we must become part of a sound congregation so we can meet with others and can all encourage one another and serve God together (cf. Acts 9:26; Hebrews 10:25).

The Value of the Kingdom

According to Jesus' parable, His kingdom is worth more than all that we have or could hope to have. This is why the man was willing to sell "*all that he had*" in order to obtain it (Matthew 13:46). It is worth more than all the "*fine pearls*" (Matthew 13:45) this man was seeking because he gave up his search once he found this "*one pearl of great value.*"

The kingdom is valuable because it was purchased with the blood of Christ (Acts 20:28). Peter described this as "*precious blood*" that is more valuable than "*perishable things like silver or gold*" (1 Peter 1:18-19). Jesus' blood is precious because it alone is able to "*cleanse your conscience from dead works to serve the living God*" (Hebrews 9:14). The kingdom was valuable enough that Jesus willingly shed His blood on the cross in order to purchase it.

Paul showed the value of the kingdom in his willingness to suffer for it. He told Timothy, "*For this reason I endure all things for the sake of those who are chosen*" (2 Timothy 2:10). Who are the "*chosen*"? They are those who are saved and in the kingdom. He emphasized the need for Christians to be willing to suffer for the sake of the kingdom as well. As he went about preaching the gospel, he taught, *"Through many tribulations we must enter the kingdom of God"* (Acts 14:22). Why would anyone be willing to suffer, and encourage others to suffer, for the kingdom? It is because he understood how valuable of a treasure the kingdom was.

What We Need to Give Up

The man in Jesus' parable sold all that he had so that he might obtain the *"pearl of great value"* (Matthew 13:46). It cost him something. If we are going to become a part of Christ's kingdom – the church – it will cost us something as well.

The primary thing we must give up to be part of Christ's church is any tie that we might have to the churches of men. This will not always be easy. It certainly will not be popular. For years people have been told, "Join the church of your choice," as if every church is right before God. The reality, though, is that there is only *one* right church – the church that Jesus built (Matthew 16:18) and purchased with His blood on the cross (Acts 20:28). Jesus said, *"Every plant which My heavenly Father did not plant shall be uprooted"* (Matthew 15:13). Any church that was not built by Christ will not stand. If we are part of another church than His, we will not be saved since He is *"the Savior of the body"* (Ephesians 5:23).

Besides giving up the churches of men, which may be most obvious, we must also be willing to give up *anything* that might hinder us from entering the kingdom, such as preconceived notions, prejudice, pride, relationships, the fleshly desires often fulfilled by the "ministries" of the churches of men, etc.

Conclusion

The denominational world has brainwashed people into thinking that "one church is as good as another" so you can "join the church of your choice." What we ought to do instead is find the Lord's church – the *"pearl of great value"* (Matthew 13:46) – and become a part of it. No matter what the cost – even if we must sell everything as the man in Jesus' parable – it is worth it. It is only in Christ's church that salvation is found (Acts 2:47; Ephesians 5:23).

Questions for Discussion & Reflection

1. What is the kingdom and how is it related to the church?

2. Where can we find a description of the kingdom?

3. What is the universal church and how does one become part of it?

4. What is the local church and how can we identify it?

5. With what was the church purchased? How does this help us understand the value of the kingdom?

6. What must we be willing to give up in order to be part of Christ's kingdom?

The Great Gain of Godliness

Why do we serve God? Different people will have different answers to that question. Yet not all of them will have the right motivation. Some are motivated by *material* gain – a better life now. We sometimes use the term "health and wealth gospel" to refer to the message that is tailored to this group's desires. Others are motivated by *spiritual* gain – a better life in eternity. Many are motivated by a combination of the two. In this lesson, we will consider Paul's words to Timothy in which he warned of the danger of being motivated by material gain and he explained what is the great gain of godliness.

> *"But godliness actually is a means of great gain when accompanied by contentment"* (1 Timothy 6:6).

The Error of the "Health and Wealth Gospel"

Paul warned Timothy that some would preach a *"different doctrine"* that *"does not agree with sound words"* (1 Timothy 6:3). Any message that does not conform to the truth of God's word is false (cf. Galatians 1:6-9; 1 John 4:6). Truth is not subjective. It does not change to accommodate any culture, region, generation, or any other variable. God's word is truth (John 17:17) and anything contrary to it is false.

Notice how Paul described the false teacher he was warning Timothy about. First, he said the false teacher was *"conceited"* (1 Timothy 6:4). This evaluation was not unfair, but was based upon evidence. The fact that he taught a *"different doctrine"* was proof that he did not approach the word of God in humility as he should have (James 1:21). Second, the false teacher *"understands nothing"* (1 Timothy 6:4). One without a proper understanding of God's word will turn *"aside to fruitless discussions"* because he is not qualified to teach (1 Timothy 1:6-7). Third, the false teacher causes division (cf. Jude 18-19) as his message produces *"strife"* and *"constant friction"* (1 Timothy 6:4-5). These characteristics are true of *every* false teacher, not just the specific ones Paul warned Timothy about.

The specific false doctrine that Paul addressed is the one that said, *"Godliness is a means of gain"* (1 Timothy 6:5). The context clearly indicates that the gain promised by the false teacher was *material*. In other words, Paul was warning Timothy about those who would preach what we often call the "health and wealth gospel." Nowhere in the New Testament are we promised a better life here for being a Christian. In fact, we are promised just the opposite. The life of a Christian is a life of **sacrifice** (*"for* [Christ] *I have suffered the loss of all things"* – Philippians 3:8), **suffering** (*"if anyone suffers as a Christian, he is not to be ashamed, but is to glorify God in this name"* – 1 Peter 4:16), and **surrender** (*"Be faithful until death, and I will give you the crown of life"* – Revelation 2:10).

Of course, we must remember that God is the source of every good blessing (James 1:17). Some Christians will even be prosperous (1 Timothy 6:17). Even still, material prosperity is not the promise or the goal of the gospel.

The Gain of Godliness

Though there is no promise of material wealth as a reward for godliness, there is something to be gained. Paul said, *"But godliness actually is a means of great gain"* (1 Timothy 6:6). So what is the gain of godliness?

Paul gave a clue about the gain of godliness in the next verse: *"For we have brought nothing into the world, so we cannot take anything out of it either"* (1 Timothy 6:7). The gain of godliness is for something past this life. Paul said elsewhere, *"If we have hoped in Christ in this life only, we are of all men most to be pitied"* (1 Corinthians 15:19). If our hope lies beyond this life, what do we stand to gain?

- **A home in heaven** – Jesus told His disciples, *"In My Father's house are many dwelling places; if it were not so, I would have told you; for I go to prepare a place for you. If I go and prepare a place for you, I will come again and receive you to Myself, that where I am, there you may be also"* (John 14:2-3). As part of Christ's kingdom, *"our citizenship is in heaven"* (Philippians 3:20). The home we hope to gain for following Christ is not a bigger house in this world, but is a dwelling place in heaven.
- **Eternal life** – In speaking of the need for His followers to sacrifice, Jesus said, *"And everyone who has left houses or brothers or sisters or father or mother or children or farms for My name's sake, will receive many times as much, and will inherit eternal life"* (Matthew 19:29). The home of heaven that we seek is not a place where we will live for a few years – even a thousand years – and then will

have to leave. Life in heaven will be *eternal*. Everything of this life is only temporary.

- **The chance to be in the presence of God** – When Paul sought to encourage the brethren in Thessalonica about their fellow Christians who had already passed from this life, he told them of what would happen when the Lord returns: *"For the Lord Himself will descend from heaven with a shout, with the voice of the archangel and with the trumpet of God, and the dead in Christ will rise first. Then we who are alive and remain will be caught up together with them in the clouds to meet the Lord in the air, and so we shall always be with the Lord. Therefore comfort one another with these words"* (1 Thessalonians 4:16-18). Faithful Christians, regardless of whether they are living or dead, will one day be in the presence of God. These words are a source of comfort when a fellow Christian passes away. They are also a source of encouragement at all times as we can look ahead to our eternal home in heaven with the One who loved us enough to save us from our sins.

As we come to understand the great gain of godliness, it is important that we also know what godliness is.

What Is Godliness?

Paul warned Timothy that some would hold a mere *"form of godliness"* (2 Timothy 3:5). We need to have *real* godliness instead. So what is godliness?

The most basic definition of godliness is to be *like God*. To know God the Father, we must know Christ. John wrote,

"No one has seen God at any time; the only begotten God who is in the bosom of the Father, He has explained Him" (John 1:18). The *"only begotten God"* to Whom John referred was Jesus. If we want to know what it means to be like God, we simply need to look to Jesus. He left us *"an example"* that we might *"follow in His steps"* (1 Peter 2:21). That example was one of perfect obedience to the will of the Father (1 Peter 2:22; Hebrews 5:8; Philippians 2:8). To live godly, we must seek to obey God in all things, just as Jesus did while on earth.

Related to the above point, another definition of godliness is *living according to God's standard.* Just before he told Timothy that *"godliness actually is a means of great gain"* (1 Timothy 6:6), Paul said that *"sound words"* are part of the *"doctrine conforming to godliness"* (1 Timothy 6:3). Paul told Titus that *"truth...is according to godliness"* (Titus 1:1). Peter said that God has *"granted to us everything pertaining to life and godliness, through the true knowledge of Him who called us"* (2 Peter 1:3). To live godly, we must know God's standard (His word) and conform our lives to it.

The Need of Contentment

It is important to note what Paul said about the role of contentment in this: *"But godliness actually is a means of great gain when accompanied by contentment"* (1 Timothy 6:6). The things of this life are only temporary – they are uncertain (1 Timothy 6:17), corruptible (Matthew 6:19), and will be destroyed (2 Peter 3:10). Like Paul, we need to be *"content in whatever circumstances"* we find ourselves (Philippians 4:11). Regardless of our circumstances, our lives are *"just a vapor that appears for a little while and then vanishes away"* (James 4:14). We must not allow a lack of contentment to cause us to become distracted by the things of this life that we lose the gain of godliness.

Therefore, Paul went on to warn against the love of money: "*But those who want to get rich fall into temptation and a snare and many foolish and harmful desires which plunge men into ruin and destruction. For the love of money is a root of all sorts of evil, and some by longing for it have wandered away from the faith and pierced themselves with many griefs*" (1 Timothy 6:9-10). This warning is for us all – rich and poor – to not allow either the desire for or the pursuit of earthly wealth to cloud our vision of the far greater gain of godliness.

Conclusion

The Lord offers us a great reward for living godly lives. Let us not lose sight of His reward by focusing on either the false promises of false teachers, or our own desire for this world's goods. Let us live godly lives so that we can be with God for eternity.

Questions for Discussion & Reflection

1. What must godliness be coupled with if it is to be a means of great gain for us?

2. What is the "health and wealth gospel"?

3. Why is the "health and wealth gospel" a false doctrine?

4. What do we hope to gain by living godly lives?

5. Define godliness.

6. Is the warning against "the love of money" directed only at the rich? Explain.

A Counterfeit Spirituality

When the Lord addressed the church at Laodicea, He condemned them for practicing a spirituality that was not of the Lord, but was *counterfeit*. Therefore, He advised these brethren who thought they needed nothing to buy certain things from Him so that they might have a *real* spirituality.

> "*I know your deeds, that you are neither cold nor hot; I wish that you were cold or hot. So because you are lukewarm, and neither hot nor cold, I will spit you out of My mouth. Because you say, 'I am rich, and have become wealthy, and have need of nothing,' and you do not know that you are wretched and miserable and poor and blind and naked, I advise you to buy from Me gold refined by fire so that you may become rich, and white garments so that you may clothe yourself, and that the shame of your nakedness will not be revealed; and eye salve to anoint your eyes so that you may see*" (Revelation 3:15-18).

A "Lukewarm" Spirituality

The problem with the church in Laodicea was that it was filled with "*lukewarm*" Christians. What does it mean that they were "*lukewarm*"? They were just spiritual enough to be comfortable. They were not completely devoted to the Lord as He demands. In repeating the requirement given in the Old Law, Jesus said, "*You shall love the Lord your God with all your heart, and with all your soul, and with all your mind*" (Matthew 22:37). We are to offer ourselves as *living sacrifices* (Romans 12:1; cf. Luke 9:23). This is only possible with a wholehearted devotion to the Lord.

Why was the spirituality of the Laodiceans' so shallow? Notice how Jesus described their mindset: "*You say, 'I am rich, and have become wealthy, and have need of nothing*" (Revelation 3:17). Their wealth had deceived them into thinking they were self-sufficient. They were blind to the fact that they were sorely lacking spiritually. A "*lukewarm*" spirituality is one that is derived from the things of this world. The only way to fix the problem and to exchange this counterfeit spirituality for the real thing is to buy the three things Jesus tells these brethren they were to buy.

Gold Refined by Fire

Real spirituality focuses on the *true* riches that are offered to us in Christ. When gold is refined by fire, it is purified, thereby making it more valuable. The gold offered to the Laodiceans represents the *true* riches in Christ. In Christ is where all spiritual blessings are found (Ephesians 1:3). What are these blessings? Notice a few of them below:

- **The adoption as sons** – "*In love He predestined us to adoption as sons through Jesus Christ to Himself*" (Ephesians 1:5). In Christ we have the opportunity to be "*called children of God*" (1 John 3:1). We can "*cry out, 'Abba! Father!'*" (Romans

8:15) because of this close relationship with Him. All of this is made possible *"through Jesus Christ"* (Ephesians 1:5).

- **Redemption, forgiveness, and grace** – *"In Him we have redemption through His blood, the forgiveness of our trespasses, according to the riches of His grace"* (Ephesians 1:7). All men have sinned and are worthy of death (Romans 3:23; 6:23). Through the sacrifice of Christ, we have the opportunity to be forgiven and restored to a right relationship with God.
- **The revelation of God's will** – *"He made known to us the mystery of His will, according to His kind intention which He purposed in Him"* (Ephesians 1:9). Jesus is the spokesman for the new covenant (Hebrews 1:2). He came to *"testify to the truth"* (John 18:37). His words show us the way to eternal life (John 6:68).
- **An inheritance** – *"Also we have obtained an inheritance, having been predestined according to His purpose who works all things after the counsel of His will"* (Ephesians 1:11). This inheritance is described by Peter as being *"imperishable and undefiled and will not fade away, reserved in heaven for you"* (1 Peter 1:4).

Counterfeit spirituality seeks to find these spiritual blessings *apart from Christ*, or in a *different form* than they are found in Christ.

- **The adoption as sons** – Rather than seeking to be children of God through Christ (Ephesians 1:5), many claim to be children of God *apart from Christ*. The Jews claimed this in the first century.

Yet Paul explained that they were only *"Abraham's descendants"* if they belonged *"to Christ"* (Galatians 3:29). We are only children of God *"through Jesus Christ"* (Ephesians 1:5).

- **Redemption, forgiveness, and grace** – Many believe that one can be saved (and reach heaven) outside of Christ. But Jesus did not say He was *a* way; He said He was *the* way (John 14:6). Peter said, *"There is no other name under heaven that has been given among men by which we must be saved"* (Acts 4:12). Of course, the name to which he was referring was the name of *Christ*.

- **The revelation of God's will** – The *"mind of Christ"* has been revealed by the Spirit through the word of God (1 Corinthians 2:10-16). This word is what produces faith in us today (Romans 10:17). But many are not content with this. So they foolishly seek after the opinions, philosophies, traditions, and creeds of men; contrary to what we ought to do (cf. Galatians 1:6-9; Colossians 2:8, 23; Matthew 15:6-9).

- **An inheritance** – Many believe the inheritance offered through Christ refers to the riches of this life [see previous lesson]. Some think it is to be part of a *physical* kingdom of Christ *on the earth*. Yet the inheritance is *clearly* in heaven, not on the earth (1 Peter 1:4). And it certainly does not involve a better life here, as Paul said, *"If we have hoped in Christ in this life only, we are of all men most to be pitied"* (1 Corinthians 15:19). Without Christ, we are as the Lord described the Laodiceans: *"wretched and miserable and poor and blind and naked"* (Revelation 3:17).

White Garments

Real spirituality focuses on obtaining spiritual garments of white that are offered by Christ. The *"white garments"* symbolize *purity*. We first obtain these garments when we become pure and forgiven of sin in the waters of baptism (Acts 2:38; 22:16). Yet many have a counterfeit spirituality since they have been convinced that they can be forgiven and obtain these *"white garments"* before and without water baptism.

Real spirituality also seeks to keep the spiritual garments of the soul pure and unstained by sin. We are to *"walk in the Light as He Himself is in the Light"* (1 John 1:7). Christians are to be different from the world – not *conformed*, but *transformed* (Romans 12:2). Christians are not to be "just a bunch of sinners" (cf. 1 John 1:6). People should be able to *see* the difference between our lives and the lives of those in the world (1 Peter 4:3-4). We may sin occasionally, but those with a real spirituality will not be constantly mired in sin (Romans 6:11-14).

Counterfeit spirituality embraces the garments of the old man (Colossians 3:5-9) – those that have been *"polluted by the flesh"* (Jude 23). Those who accept this form of spirituality believe that the righteous – those who clothe themselves with *"white garments"* by following the Lord – are merely self-righteous hypocrites. After all, how could someone truly live righteously when we are all human and cannot help but sin? The problem is that the righteous are not being accused for their own sin, but are being unjustly accused for the sins of their accusers. The fact is, the Bible tells us that there is a way that we can *"never stumble"* (2 Peter 1:10) as God has promised a *"way of escape"* for every temptation (1 Corinthians 10:13). We are to strive for perfection (Matthew 5:48) as we "*consider* [ourselves] *to be dead to sin, but alive to God*" (Romans 6:11). Those who have a false spirituality in claiming to be "just a sinner" need to quit sinning and repent. Samuel told Saul: "*Behold, to obey is better than sacrifice*" (1 Samuel 15:22).

Eye Salve

Real spirituality focuses on seeing things the way God sees them. We are to judge, not with our own flawed judgment, but "*with righteous judgment*" (John 7:24). We are to test ourselves according to the faith (2 Corinthians 13:5), not according to our opinion. Real spirituality involves an honest, unbiased, unprejudiced perspective, so that we can look at ourselves clearly in the mirror of God's word (James 1:23-25).

Counterfeit spirituality focuses on what one is able to see and experience with his eyes. It causes one to "walk by sight and not by faith" (cf. 2 Corinthians 5:7). It causes one to go after the "*way which seems right to a man, but its end is the way of death*" (Proverbs 14:12).

Conclusion

A counterfeit spirituality – like what the Laodiceans had – leads one to conform his religion to his physical senses and desires. We must rise above this, or else the Lord will "*spit* [us] *out of* [His] *mouth*" (Revelation 3:16). We must have a *real* spirituality that values the spiritual blessings in Christ and is careful to remain pure before God. If we do this we can enjoy fellowship with the Lord (Revelation 3:21-22 – *we will dine with Him and sit with Him on His throne).* Otherwise, in the end, He will have nothing to do with us.

Questions for Discussion & Reflection

1. In a spiritual sense, what does it mean to be "lukewarm"?

2. What was it that caused the spirituality of the Laodiceans to be so shallow?

3. What are the riches that can be found in Christ?

4. What counterfeit riches does the religious world focus on?

5. Explain the significance of "white garments." How do we receive them and keep them clean?

6. How does God want us to see things?

Faith More Precious Than Gold

The next and final lesson in our series will deal with the *"treasures in heaven"* (Matthew 6:20). But before we get to that, we must answer this question: How can we make it through the trials of life so that we will reach heaven? The answer to this question is that we will *"obtain an inheritance...in heaven [...] through faith"* (1 Peter 1:4-5). Peter went on to describe the value of a *proven* faith.

> *"In this you greatly rejoice, even though now for a little while, if necessary, you have been distressed by various trials, so that the proof of your faith, being more precious than gold which is perishable, even though tested by fire, may be found to result in praise and glory and honor at the revelation of Jesus Christ"* (1 Peter 1:6-7).

The Bible Definition of Faith

When we talk about *faith*, we need to understand it in the way the Bible defines it, rather than in the way the religious world at large defines it. Faith is not merely a belief in the existence of God. James said, *"The demons...believe"* (James 2:19), but they did not have *faith*. So what is faith? The Hebrew writer described it so that we might understand:

"Now faith is the assurance [substance, KJV] of things hoped for, the conviction [evidence, KJV] of things not seen" (Hebrews 11:1).

"And without faith it is impossible to please Him, for he who comes to God must believe that He is and that He is a rewarder of those who seek Him" (Hebrews 11:6).

These verses tell us a few things about faith. First, we have faith regarding things we *hope for* – namely the reward of heaven. Second, faith is about things *not seen* (cf. 2 Corinthians 5:7 – *"For we walk by faith, not by sight"*). Third, those unseen things for which we hope are not unrealistic fantasies. They are based upon *evidence*. God does not expect us to take a "leap of faith" – choosing to believe something against our better judgment – but to be convicted and assured based upon what He has revealed to us. Fourth, faith involves belief in the existence of God. Fifth, faith involves belief in the power of God – that He is able to reward us. Sixth, faith involves the understanding of our need to *seek* God. This is not a mere mental acknowledgement of the existence of God. This is a desire to actively pursue God (obedience and godly living).

Understanding now what faith is, how do we get faith? Some mistakenly believe that one can only have faith if the Holy Spirit performs some sort of direct operation on his heart. This is false. The Bible tells us how to obtain faith: *"So faith comes from hearing, and hearing by the word of Christ"* (Romans 10:17). We have faith today based upon what has been revealed in the Scriptures.

There Will Be Trials in Life

Peter told the Christians to whom he wrote that they had been *"distressed by various trials"* (1 Peter 1:6). It is true that all men – whether they are followers of God or not – will have trouble in life (Job 14:1). Yet the trials to which Peter referred are not the general hardships of life that everyone faces. These are trials that are peculiar to Christians. Notice what he wrote later in this epistle:

> *"Beloved, do not be surprised at the fiery ordeal among you, which comes upon you for your testing, as though some strange thing were happening to you; but to the degree that you share the sufferings of Christ, keep on rejoicing, so that also at the revelation of His glory you may rejoice with exultation. If you are reviled for the name of Christ, you are blessed, because the Spirit of glory and of God rests on you. Make sure that none of you suffers as a murderer, or thief, or evildoer, or a troublesome meddler; but if anyone suffers as a Christian, he is not to be ashamed, but is to glorify God in this name"* (1 Peter 4:12-16).

Peter made it clear that the *"various trials"* that distress us (1 Peter 1:6) are trials we suffer *for our faith in Christ*. We *"share the sufferings of Christ"* (1 Peter 4:13). We are *"reviled for the name of Christ"* (1 Peter 4:14). We suffer *as Christians* (1 Peter 4:16). This suffering was not unique to the Christians who originally received Peter's letter. Paul told Timothy, *"Indeed, all who desire to live godly in Christ Jesus will be persecuted"* (2 Timothy 3:12).

We will, of course, face the general hardships of life as all men do. But in addition to these, we will also suffer as Christians. Though the type and severity of persecution will vary with time, place, and other factors, being targeted for suffering will be a reality for all of God's people.

Our Faith Must Be Proven

Faith is essential for salvation (Hebrews 11:6). But if our faith is not strong enough to sustain us through the inevitable trials of life, it will not do us any good. In light of the persecution they would be facing, Jesus told the church in Smyrna, *"Be faithful until death, and I will give you the crown of life"* (Revelation 2:10). It would not be enough for them to be faithful only when times were good and peace prevailed. Their faith needed to be proven through trials. He said in the next verse, *"He who overcomes will not be hurt by the second death"* (Revelation 2:11).

In the parable of the sower, Jesus spoke of four different types of soils (Luke 8:5-8). These represented four different types of hearts that would be taught the gospel (Luke 8:11-15). The rocky soil represents those who have an unproven faith that will not endure under trial. Notice the parable and the Lord's explanation:

> *"Other seed fell on rocky soil, and as soon as it grew up, it withered away, because it had no moisture"* (Luke 8:6).

> *"Those on the rocky soil are those who, when they hear, receive the word with joy; and these have no firm root; they believe for a while, and in time of temptation fall away"* (Luke 8:13).

Initially, those who are represented by the rocky soil will accept the gospel and begin to grow. But this will be short-lived. When it becomes difficult to remain faithful – whether it is due to persecution, intimidation, peer pressure, or any other reason – many will fall away. One with *"an honest and good heart"* will *"bear fruit with perseverance"* (Luke 8:15). One with a shallow faith will only bear a little fruit (if any) when it is convenient.

The proof of one's faith is not about what one says or does when it is convenient. Our faith must be proven through *"various trials"* (1 Peter 1:6-7). Peter later wrote, *"Therefore, since Christ has suffered in the flesh, arm yourselves also with the same purpose, because he who has suffered in the flesh has ceased from sin"* (1 Peter 4:1). Jesus suffered and died on the cross for us. If we believe that, we must put our faith into practice and be willing to suffer for Him. Jesus said, *"If anyone wishes to come after Me, he must deny himself, and take up his cross daily and follow Me"* (Luke 9:23). Paul wrote, *"Therefore, I urge you, brethren, by the mercies of God, to present your bodies a living and holy sacrifice"* (Romans 12:1). We cannot claim to be living sacrifices if we forsake the Lord at any moment it seems that our faith may cause us to suffer. Willingness to suffer is evidence of a genuine faith.

The Result of a Proven Faith

What is the result of our faith being proven under trial? Notice a few passages:

> *"Consider it all joy, my brethren, when you encounter various trials, knowing that the testing of your faith produces endurance. And*

let endurance have its perfect result, so that you may be perfect and complete, lacking in nothing" (James 1:2-4; cf. 1 Peter 5:10).

"Blessed are those who have been persecuted for the sake of righteousness, for theirs is the kingdom of heaven" (Matthew 5:10).

"So that the proof of your faith, being more precious than gold which is perishable, even though tested by fire, may be found to result in praise and glory and honor at the revelation of Jesus Christ" (1 Peter 1:7; cf. Romans 8:17).

"Do not fear what you are about to suffer. Behold, the devil is about to cast some of you into prison, so that you will be tested, and you will have tribulation for ten days. Be faithful until death, and I will give you the crown of life" (Revelation 2:10; cf. James 1:12).

There are other passages that could also be cited. But just from those listed above, we can see the great benefit of a proven faith – one that endures in the face of trials – and why Peter said it is *"more precious than gold"* (1 Peter 1:7). A proven faith leads to endurance; perfection; completeness; citizenship in Christ's kingdom; praise, glory, and honor at the Lord's return; and, ultimately, a crown of life in heaven.

Conclusion

When James addressed the erroneous belief that one could be saved by *"faith alone"* (James 2:24), he gave a simple test whereby one could *prove* his faith. *"But someone may well say, 'You have faith and I have works; show me your faith without the works, and I will show you my faith by my works'* (James 2:18). One of the "works" we must do to demonstrate our faith is to willingly suffer for the cause of Christ. If we are unwilling to endure various trials for Christ, then the faith we have is a dead faith (James 2:17, 26), not a saving faith.

———————————

Questions for Discussion & Reflection

1. What is faith?

2. Explain why the "leap of faith" concept is not Biblical.

3. Should we be surprised if we suffer for our faith? Explain.

4. Explain the type of faith represented by the rocky soil in Jesus' parable (Luke 8:6, 13).

5. What does it mean to present our bodies as living sacrifices (Romans 12:1)?

6. What is produced from a proven faith?

~7~

Treasures in Heaven

This is the final lesson in our series in which we have been discussing what the Bible describes as wise investments. They are things of great value – not valuable from a material standpoint, but valuable because they pertain to that which is spiritual and eternal. In this last lesson, we will consider what ought to be the goal of all of our efforts – a home in heaven.

> "*Do not store up for yourselves treasures on earth, where moth and rust destroy, and where thieves break in and steal. But store up for yourselves treasures in heaven, where neither moth nor rust destroys, and where thieves do not break in or steal; for where your treasure is, there your heart will be also*" (Matthew 6:19-21).

Where Will We Choose to Have Our Home?

When Jesus told his audience not to store up treasures on earth, but rather to store up treasures in heaven, He implied that they were free to choose one option or the other. We can choose to go to heaven. No one can stop us if we wish to go. Contrary to what the adherents of Calvinism believe, heaven is not just for an arbitrarily chosen few. Paul said, "*For the grace of God has appeared, bringing salvation to all men*" (Titus 2:11). This does not mean that all will be saved (Matthew 7:13-14). Instead, it means that all who meet God's conditions of grace will be saved – belief (John 8:24; Hebrews 11:6), repentance (Luke 13:3, 5; 2 Peter 3:9), confession (Romans 10:9-10), baptism (Acts 2:38; 1 Peter 3:21), and a life of faithfulness (Revelation 2:10). This is why Jesus told His apostles, "*Go into all the world and preach the gospel to all creation. He who has believed and has been baptized shall be saved; but he who has disbelieved shall be condemned*" (Mark 16:15-16). This message of hope through faithful obedience to the gospel of Christ was not for a select few; it was – and still is – for *all*.

Will we choose to go to heaven? Will we meet the conditions of God's grace? Will we "*store up...treasures in heaven*" (Matthew 6:20)? God does not *force* us to obey Him so that we will go to heaven. Instead, He *persuades* us through the preaching of His word (2 Corinthians 5:11). If we are going to make a wise decision about whether to make heaven our home or not, we must weigh the options.

The Treasures of Heaven

What is there about heaven that should cause us to want to go? Notice what the Bible says about heaven:

- **We will be in the presence of God** – "*There will no longer be any curse; and the throne of God and of the Lamb will be in it, and His bond-servants will serve Him; they will see His face, and His name will be on their foreheads*" (Revelation 22:3-4). Why is this special? It is because "*God is love*" (1 John 4:8). He loved us enough to offer His Son for us (John 3:16). Because of His great goodness toward us, we cannot help but want to be in His presence.

- **We will have rest** – *"So there remains a Sabbath rest for the people of God"* (Hebrews 4:9-10). However, this rest does not come in this life but after this life. John was told, *"Blessed are the dead who die in the Lord...so that they may rest from their labors, for their deeds follow with them"* (Revelation 14:13).

- **We will have no troubles or trials** – In recording the description of heaven, John wrote, *"He will wipe away every tear from their eyes; and there will no longer be any death; there will no longer be any mourning, or crying, or pain; the first things have passed away"* (Revelation 21:4). Everything that causes sorrow on earth will be absent in heaven.

- **We will enjoy eternal life** – *"For the wages of sin is death, but the free gift of God is eternal life in Christ Jesus our Lord"* (Romans 6:23; cf. 1 John 5:11). Life on earth is *"just a vapor that appears for a little while and then vanishes away"* (James 4:14). But life in heaven will never end.

Compare these things about heaven with the alternative – hell:

- **We will be away from the presence of God** – Of the unfaithful, Paul said, *"These will pay the penalty of eternal destruction, away from the presence of the Lord and from the glory of His power"* (2 Thessalonians 1:9). Since God is the source of light (1 John 1:5; Revelation 21:23), the place away from His presence is a place of *"outer* *darkness*" (Matthew 25:30).

- **We will have no rest** – "*And the smoke of their torment goes up forever and ever; they have no rest day and night, those who worship the beast and his image, and whoever receives the mark of his name*" (Revelation 14:11).

- **We will endure pain and anguish** – While heaven is described as a place that does not have any of the sorrows of life, hell will be a place that will be far worse than anything in this life. Jesus said, "*In that place there will be weeping and gnashing of teeth*" (Matthew 25:30).

- **We will suffer eternal torment** – The punishment of hell is not temporary, nor is it a quick annihilation as some believe. Instead, it will be equal to heaven in its duration. Jesus said, "*These will go away into eternal punishment, but the righteous into eternal life*" (Matthew 25:46). Those who are lost will suffer "*the punishment of eternal fire*" (Jude 7), and "*the smoke of their torment* [will go] *up forever and ever*" (Revelation 14:11).

After making this comparison between heaven and hell, the wise choice should be obvious. We must choose *heaven* as our home!

This World is Not Our Home

In the previous point, we contrasted heaven and hell. Yet in our text, Jesus contrasted "*treasures in heaven*" with "*treasures on earth*" (Matthew 6:19-21). Why does Jesus make this comparison? It is because this is the comparison that the devil will make. No one in his right mind will choose hell over heaven. But some will choose the here and now over the hereafter. The prosperous land owner of Jesus' parable did this. He said, *"I will tear down my barns and build larger ones, and there I will store all my grain and my goods. And I will say to my soul, 'Soul, you have many goods laid up for many years to come; take your ease, eat, drink and be merry'"* (Luke 12:18-19). His problem was not in his prosperity, but that he neglected the state of his soul so he could focus on the things of this life.

When the rich young ruler came to Jesus, he asked, *"Teacher, what good thing shall I do that I may obtain eternal life?"* (Matthew 19:16). His question was a good one. Jesus told him, *"Go and sell your possessions and give to the poor, and you will have treasure in heaven; and come, follow Me"* (Matthew 19:21). Yet this man was unwilling to do this: *"But when the young man heard this statement, he went away grieving; for he was one who owned much property"* (Matthew 19:22). He was unwilling to part with the treasures of earth he valued so highly in order to gain the treasures of heaven that were far more valuable.

We need to remember that we are *"aliens and strangers"* in this world (1 Peter 2:11) and that *"our citizenship is in heaven"* (Philippians 3:20). Whatever we may gain in this life is only temporary, as it is part of the world which is *"passing away"* (1 John 2:17) and will in the end *"be destroyed with intense heat"* (2 Peter 3:10). No treasure on earth can compare with the treasure stored up in heaven for the faithful.

What is Important to Us?

Are we pursing spiritual and eternal things, or material and temporal things? This is really the main question in all of the lessons in this series.

- Are we seeking to save our souls, or are we striving to better our lives here at all costs (Matthew 16:26)?
- Are we diligently pursuing the truth, or are we choosing to accept the way that seems right to man (Proverbs 23:23; 14:12)?
- Are we seeking the kingdom of God, or are we content with the churches of men (Matthew 13:45-46)?
- Are we striving to obtain the great gain of godliness, or are we hoping for this world's wealth as our reward (1 Timothy 6:5-6)?
- Are we trying to have a real spirituality, or do we have a counterfeit and *"lukewarm"* spirituality (Revelation 3:15-18)?
- Are we allowing our faith to be proven, or are we compromising our faith when it is convenient to do so (1 Peter 1:6-7)?
- Are we laying up treasures in heaven, or are we focused too much on the treasures of earth (Matthew 6:19-21)?

We need to have the right perspective and be willing to make the proper sacrifices in order to gain those things which are worth obtaining.

Conclusion

We must be convinced that those things we have discussed in this series are more important than the things of this world. In order to do this, we must *"walk by faith, not by sight"* (2 Corinthians 5:7). The things we should value most highly are not material and temporal, but rather are spiritual and eternal. Remember the words of the Hebrew writer:

> *"And without faith it is impossible to please Him, for he who comes to God must believe that He is and that He is a rewarder of those who seek Him"* (Hebrews 11:6).

If we seek God in faith, we will be rewarded when the Lord returns (Revelation 22:12). Therefore, let us not lose sight of what is truly important, so that we might reap the benefits of these wise investments.

Questions for Discussion & Reflection

1. Why did Jesus warn against laying up treasures on earth?

2. What must we *do* in order to lay up treasures in heaven?

3. What is it about heaven that makes it valuable?

4. Explain how the conditions in hell are the opposite of those in heaven.

5. Why did Jesus contrast *"treasures in heaven"* with *"treasures on earth"*?

6. As Christians, what is our relationship with the world? Why it is important that we remember this?

Other Books by the Author

NEW – *Take Courage: Eight Lessons from Men of Faith*

We live in difficult times. It can be tempting for Christians to compromise their principles and abandon their faith. Yet, as Jesus told His apostles, we must *take courage* (John 16:33). To help us see *how* we can take courage today, this book contains eight lessons from men of faith to see what we can learn from their examples.

NEW – *Bringing Up Children in the Lord*

The topic of parenting is vital – not only for the Lord's church, but also for society as a whole. Children are the future; therefore, it is important that parents take their responsibility seriously to bring up their children in the right way. This book contains a 6-lesson study on the topic of parenting.

My Son, Hear My Words: Notes on Proverbs

This book arranges the verses in Proverbs by topic and then provides commentary on the text. The commentary in this book is a valuable reference tool as you seek to learn and apply the teachings in the book of Proverbs. Its topical arrangement also makes it useful for personal and group Bible studies.

Daily Notes & Observations

This book contains 365 Scripture-based articles on a wide range of topics, taken from every area of the word of God. These articles, as well as the Bible reading plans and spaces for your notes, are designed to encourage a regular habit of studying and meditating upon the Scriptures.

For more information about these books, as well as other helpful materials, visit www.GospelArmory.com.

Made in the USA
Columbia, SC
16 February 2023

12492207R00040